Let It Go

Journal

INTRODUCTION

Welcome to your Let It Go journal. This is a safe space for you to be completely honest with yourself, without fear of judgment or consequences. The pages of this journal are meant to be burned (or torn) after you write on them, which allows you to release any pent-up emotions or thoughts you may have been holding onto.

This journal is a personal space for you to explore your innermost thoughts and feelings. It is a place to ask yourself hard questions, to challenge yourself, and to grow. Whether you use it to process difficult emotions, to work through personal issues, or simply to reflect on your life, this journal is a powerful tool for self-discovery.

Each page of this journal is a blank canvas, waiting for you to pour your heart out onto it. There are no rules, no expectations, and no limits. You have complete freedom to express yourself in whatever way feels most authentic to you.

Remember, this journal is for your eyes only. You don't have to share your thoughts or feelings with anyone else unless you choose to. You can be as open and vulnerable as you want to be, knowing that you are in a safe and supportive environment.

So take a deep breath, pick up your pen, and let your thoughts flow onto the pages of this Burn After Writing journal. You might be surprised at what you discover about yourself along the way.

Please note that, if you can't find a safe place or way to burn the pages, please just tear them into pieces instead of burning them. Always take safety measures into account while burning the pages.

What is your biggest fear?

Write about a time when you felt the loneliest.

What is something you've never told anyone?

What are you running away from?

Write about a time you were betrayed.

What is your deepest regret?

Write a letter to your past self.

What would you say to the person who hurt you the most?

What are you ashamed of?

What is the biggest lie you have ever told?

Write about a time when you were rejected.

What is something you wish you could forget?

What is something you wish you could
change about yourself?

Write a letter to your younger self.

What is your biggest insecurity?

Write about a time when you failed.

What is something you've always wanted to do but haven't?

What is your biggest secret?

Write about a time when you felt lost.

What is something you've been holding onto for too long?

Write about a time when you felt like giving up.

What is something you're afraid to admit to yourself?

What is your biggest disappointment?

What is something you wish someone would tell you?

Write about a time when you felt invisible.

What is your biggest regret in a past relationship?

Write about a time when you were judged unfairly.

What is something you wish you could have said to someone?

What is your biggest mistake?

Write a letter to someone who has hurt you.

What is something you've never forgiven yourself for?

What is your biggest weakness?

Write about a time when you were heartbroken.

What is something you're afraid to face?

What is something you wish you could do differently?

What is your biggest secret fantasy?

Write about a time when you were taken advantage of.

What is something you've been pretending not to know?

What is your biggest regret in your career?

Write about a time when you felt rejected by society.

What is something you wish you could change about
the world?

Write about a time when you felt like giving up on your
dreams.

What is your biggest insecurity in your relationships?

What is your biggest regret in your life so far?

The pages are all yours now. Write anything that is worrying or bothering you or eating you up on the inside. Vent on the pages and then either burn them or tear them apart.